CLUE
MAD LIBS®

by

MAD LIBS
An Imprint of Penguin Random House LLC, New York

Mad Libs format copyright © 2020 by Penguin Random House LLC.
All rights reserved.

Concept created by Roger Price & Leonard Stern

HASBRO and its logo, CLUE and all related characters are trademarks of Hasbro
and are used with permission. © 2020 Hasbro. All Rights Reserved.

Published by Mad Libs,
an imprint of Penguin Random House LLC, New York.
Printed in the USA.

Visit us online at www.penguinrandomhouse.com.

ISBN 9780593222089
1 3 5 7 9 10 8 6 4 2

MAD☺LIBS®

INSTRUCTIONS

MAD LIBS® is a game for people who don't like games! It can be played by one, two, three, four, or forty.

• RIDICULOUSLY SIMPLE DIRECTIONS

In this tablet you will find stories containing blank spaces where words are left out. One player, the READER, selects one of these stories. The READER does not tell anyone what the story is about. Instead, he/she asks the other players, the WRITERS, to give him/her words. These words are used to fill in the blank spaces in the story.

• TO PLAY

The READER asks each WRITER in turn to call out a word—an adjective or a noun or whatever the space calls for—and uses them to fill in the blank spaces in the story. The result is a MAD LIBS® game.

When the READER then reads the completed MAD LIBS® game to the other players, they will discover that they have written a story that is fantastic, screamingly funny, shocking, silly, crazy, or just plain dumb—depending upon which words each WRITER called out.

• EXAMPLE (*Before* and *After*)

"_____!" he said _____
        EXCLAMATION   ADVERB

as he jumped into his convertible _____ and
                                                      NOUN

drove off with his _____ wife.
                          ADJECTIVE

"_____OUCH_____!" he said _____HAPPILY_____
        EXCLAMATION   ADVERB

as he jumped into his convertible _____CAT_____ and
                                                      NOUN

drove off with his _____BRAVE_____ wife.
                          ADJECTIVE

In case you have forgotten what adjectives, adverbs, nouns, and verbs are, here is a quick review:

An ADJECTIVE describes something or somebody. *Lumpy, soft, ugly, messy,* and *short* are adjectives.

An ADVERB tells how something is done. It modifies a verb and usually ends in "ly." *Modestly, stupidly, greedily,* and *carefully* are adverbs.

A NOUN is the name of a person, place, or thing. *Sidewalk, umbrella, bridle, bathtub,* and *nose* are nouns.

A VERB is an action word. *Run, pitch, jump,* and *swim* are verbs. Put the verbs in past tense if the directions say PAST TENSE. *Ran, pitched, jumped,* and *swam* are verbs in the past tense.

When we ask for A PLACE, we mean any sort of place: a country or city (*Spain, Cleveland*) or a room (*bathroom, kitchen*).

An EXCLAMATION or SILLY WORD is any sort of funny sound, gasp, grunt, or outcry, like *Wow!, Ouch!, Whomp!, Ick!,* and *Gadzooks!*

When we ask for specific words, like a NUMBER, a COLOR, an ANIMAL, or a PART OF THE BODY, we mean a word that is one of those things, like *seven, blue, horse,* or *head.*

When we ask for a PLURAL, it means more than one. For example, *cat* pluralized is *cats.*

MAD LIBS® is fun to play with friends, but you can also play it by yourself! To begin with, DO NOT look at the story on the page below. Fill in the blanks on this page with the words called for. Then, using the words you have selected, fill in the blank spaces in the story.

Now you've created your own hilarious MAD LIBS® game!

GET A CLUE

EXCLAMATION _____

OCCUPATION _____

NOUN _____

PLURAL NOUN _____

NOUN _____

VERB (PAST TENSE) _____

ADJECTIVE _____

PERSON IN ROOM _____

ADJECTIVE _____

VERB _____

VERB (PAST TENSE) _____

ADJECTIVE _____

NOUN _____

NOUN _____

PLURAL NOUN _____

NUMBER _____

NUMBER _____

NOUN _____

MAD LIBS

GET A CLUE

_____ ! Mr. Boddy, the wealthy and mysterious
     EXCLAMATION

_____ and owner of Tudor Mansion, has been found
    OCCUPATION

dead as a/an _____ in his luxurious home. Now, all the
            NOUN

_____ at his dinner party are suspects. Any one of them
  PLURAL NOUN

could be the guilty _____ . But so far no one has been able
          NOUN

to figure out who _____ Mr. Boddy. The _____
     VERB (PAST TENSE)   ADJECTIVE

mystery needs to be solved, and you, _____ , are the
                    PERSON IN ROOM

_____ detective for the job! It's up to you to _____
  ADJECTIVE   VERB

out *who* among the six invited party guests _____
                                   VERB (PAST TENSE)

Mr. Boddy, *where* in the mansion's nine rooms the _____
                                    ADJECTIVE

murder took place, and *what* the killer used as a weapon to commit

this horrible _____ . Use your detective skills and follow along
        NOUN

with the stories in this _____ as we eliminate murder
                 NOUN

_____ , suspects, and rooms _____ by _____ .
  PLURAL NOUN   NUMBER   NUMBER

By the end of this _____ , will you be able to deduce . . .
               NOUN

whodunit?

From CLUE MAD LIBS® • © 2020 Hasbro. Published by Mad Libs,
an imprint of Penguin Random House LLC.

MAD LIBS® is fun to play with friends, but you can also play it by yourself! To begin with, DO NOT look at the story on the page below. Fill in the blanks on this page with the words called for. Then, using the words you have selected, fill in the blank spaces in the story.

Now you've created your own hilarious MAD LIBS® game!

IT WAS A SETUP!

ADJECTIVE _____

NOUN _____

COUNTRY _____

NUMBER _____

ADJECTIVE _____

PLURAL NOUN _____

COLOR _____

ADJECTIVE _____

NOUN _____

NOUN _____

ADJECTIVE _____

NOUN _____

EXCLAMATION _____

PLURAL NOUN _____

OCCUPATION _____

NOUN _____

MAD LIBS

IT WAS A SETUP!

The design of the Clue game board is instantly _____ . Here
  <u>ADJECTIVE</u>
are some of this classic game's most _____ -worthy features:
  <u>NOUN</u>

- The game board is designed to look like the floor plan of a 1926

  mansion in merry old _____ . It has _____ main
    <u>COUNTRY</u>   <u>NUMBER</u>

  rooms and two _____ passageways.
    <u>ADJECTIVE</u>

- Playing pieces shaped like tiny _____ represent the
    <u>PLURAL NOUN</u>

  six different murder suspects. Mr. Green is green, and Colonel

  Mustard is _____ , for example.
    <u>COLOR</u>

- Potential murder weapons are represented by _____
    <u>ADJECTIVE</u>

  props, usually made of _____ . In the original version of
    <u>NOUN</u>

  the game, the rope was made of real _____ ! Some
    <u>NOUN</u>

  _____ versions of the game even have mini-weapons
    <u>ADJECTIVE</u>

  made of gold and _____ . _____ !
    <u>NOUN</u>   <u>EXCLAMATION</u>

- Players use a deck of _____ and a/an _____ 's
    <u>PLURAL NOUN</u>   <u>OCCUPATION</u>

  notepad to track clues that help them crack the _____ !
    <u>NOUN</u>

From CLUE MAD LIBS® • © 2020 Hasbro. Published by Mad Libs,
an imprint of Penguin Random House LLC.

MAD LIBS® is fun to play with friends, but you can also play it by yourself! To begin with, DO NOT look at the story on the page below. Fill in the blanks on this page with the words called for. Then, using the words you have selected, fill in the blank spaces in the story.

Now you've created your own hilarious MAD LIBS® game!

CLUE HOW-TO

NOUN _____

CELEBRITY _____

ADJECTIVE _____

NOUN _____

NUMBER _____

NUMBER _____

OCCUPATION (PLURAL) _____

NUMBER _____

VERB _____

ADJECTIVE _____

NOUN _____

ADVERB _____

VERB _____

A PLACE _____

VERB _____

ADJECTIVE _____

VERB ENDING IN "S" _____

MAD LIBS

CLUE HOW-TO

Clue is a game that requires players to use a lot of _____ to
                                                        NOUN

solve _____'s murder. Here's some _____ rules to
        CELEBRITY   ADJECTIVE

help you crack the _____ :
                        NOUN

- You must have between three and _____ people to play the
                                        NUMBER

  game. _____ _____ cannot be on a single
          NUMBER   OCCUPATION (PLURAL)

  square at the same time, but _____ players can be in a room
                                    NUMBER

  at the same time.

- Players can either _____ the dice or use a/an _____
                          VERB   ADJECTIVE

  passage to move their character. Players can move their character

  tokens up, down, or sideways on the _____ . . . but never
                                            NOUN

  _____ .
      ADVERB

- Try to make a suggestion every time you _____ in (the)
                                                VERB

  _____ . But remember, a player can only _____
      A PLACE   VERB

  one final accusation. If any component of their accusation is

  _____ , they lose the game. However, if the accusation is
      ADJECTIVE

  correct, that player _____ !
                          VERB ENDING IN "S"

From CLUE MAD LIBS® • © 2020 Hasbro. Published by Mad Libs,
an imprint of Penguin Random House LLC.

MAD LIBS® is fun to play with friends, but you can also play it by yourself! To begin with, DO NOT look at the story on the page below. Fill in the blanks on this page with the words called for. Then, using the words you have selected, fill in the blank spaces in the story.

Now you've created your own hilarious MAD LIBS® game!

THE DETECTIVE ARRIVES!

VERB (PAST TENSE) _____

LAST NAME _____

NUMBER _____

A PLACE _____

VERB ENDING IN "ING" _____

PART OF THE BODY _____

PLURAL NOUN _____

NOUN _____

VERB _____

NUMBER _____

NOUN _____

VERB ENDING IN "ING" _____

OCCUPATION _____

ADJECTIVE _____

NOUN _____

VERB _____

VERB _____

COLOR _____

MAD LIBS

THE DETECTIVE ARRIVES!

All right, mystery solver, you have just _____ at
VERB (PAST TENSE)

Tudor Mansion. It's the middle of the night, and Mr. _____
LAST NAME

is dead. The _____ guests are roaming all over (the)
NUMBER

_____ . Everyone is _____ accusations at one
A PLACE   VERB ENDING IN "ING"

another. People are looking for _____-prints on the
PART OF THE BODY

_____ in the rooms. What a total _____! Since
PLURAL NOUN   NOUN

everyone is a suspect, you have to carefully _____ them
VERB

_____ at a time. Did the killer enter a secret _____ to
NUMBER   NOUN

sneak from room to room without anyone _____
VERB ENDING IN "ING"

them? Was the murderer a former _____ of Mr. Boddy's?
OCCUPATION

Were they a/an _____ business partner?? Could it have been
ADJECTIVE

someone who pretended to be his best _____??? Keep track of
NOUN

each clue you _____ in your investigation until you can
VERB

_____ the killer _____-handed.
VERB   COLOR

From CLUE MAD LIBS® • © 2020 Hasbro. Published by Mad Libs,
an imprint of Penguin Random House LLC.

MAD LIBS® is fun to play with friends, but you can also play it by yourself! To begin with, DO NOT look at the story on the page below. Fill in the blanks on this page with the words called for. Then, using the words you have selected, fill in the blank spaces in the story.

Now you've created your own hilarious MAD LIBS® game!

THE LIST OF SUSPECTS!

ADJECTIVE _____

TYPE OF FOOD _____

ANIMAL _____

TYPE OF EVENT (PLURAL) _____

ANIMAL _____

ADJECTIVE _____

ADJECTIVE _____

NOUN _____

OCCUPATION _____

NUMBER _____

PART OF THE BODY _____

ARTICLE OF CLOTHING (PLURAL) _____

VERB (PAST TENSE) _____

SOMETHING ALIVE _____

ADVERB _____

TYPE OF FOOD _____

NUMBER _____

PART OF THE BODY _____

MAD LIBS

THE LIST OF SUSPECTS!

One of the below suspects is _____ . But who?

ADJECTIVE

- **Professor** _____ : This book- _____ is bored to

TYPE OF FOOD   ANIMAL

  death at fancy _____ .

TYPE OF EVENT (PLURAL)

- **Mrs.** _____ : This widowed socialite may look filthy

ANIMAL

  _____ . But she'd kill for some cold, _____ cash.

ADJECTIVE   ADJECTIVE

- **Miss Scarlet:** This stunning former actress always steals the

  _____ wherever she goes.

NOUN

- **Colonel Mustard:** This former _____ fought in

OCCUPATION

  _____ wars and is a master of _____ -to-hand

NUMBER   PART OF THE BODY

  combat.

- **Dr. Orchid:** This smarty- _____ scientist

ARTICLE OF CLOTHING (PLURAL)

  was _____ out of school for creating a toxic

VERB (PAST TENSE)

  _____ . Some students got _____ sick . . .

SOMETHING ALIVE   ADVERB

  but it's not like anyone died! Or did they?

- **Mr. Green:** When he was a kid, his neighborhood _____

TYPE OF FOOD

  stand earned _____ dollars! Business is in his _____ .

NUMBER   PART OF THE BODY

MAD LIBS® is fun to play with friends, but you can also play it by yourself! To begin with, DO NOT look at the story on the page below. Fill in the blanks on this page with the words called for. Then, using the words you have selected, fill in the blank spaces in the story.

Now you've created your own hilarious MAD LIBS® game!

BAG OF TRICKS

ADJECTIVE _____

ARTICLE OF CLOTHING _____

COLOR _____

PART OF THE BODY _____

ANIMAL _____

NOUN _____

VERB ENDING IN "ING" _____

ADVERB _____

PART OF THE BODY (PLURAL) _____

VERB ENDING IN "ING" _____

NOUN _____

TYPE OF FOOD _____

VERB _____

OCCUPATION _____

ADVERB _____

VERB _____

ADJECTIVE _____

MAD LIBS

BAG OF TRICKS

You begin your detective work by spying on Mrs. Peacock, who is in

the Hall acting very _____ . Her sparkly _____
           ADJECTIVE   ARTICLE OF CLOTHING

catches your eye. Clutching her _____ satin handbag close to
                                     COLOR

her _____ , Mrs. _____ stands at a long
     PART OF THE BODY   ANIMAL

_____ near some chairs. She looks around to see if anyone is
     NOUN

_____ her and then _____ pulls a knife out
   VERB ENDING IN "ING"   ADVERB

of her purse! You can't believe your _____ . You
                                       PART OF THE BODY (PLURAL)

jump out of your _____ spot and accuse her of killing
                   VERB ENDING IN "ING"

Mr. Boddy with the razor-sharp _____ in the Hall. But just
                                   NOUN

then, she pulls a shiny red _____ out of her purse and begins
                             TYPE OF FOOD

to _____ it into slices. "Nonsense, my dear _____ ,
       VERB   OCCUPATION

I was here in the Hall when the gruesome event took place, preparing

a healthy snack," she says, _____ . Embarrassed, you shake
                               ADVERB

your head and _____ away quickly. Clearly, Mrs. Peacock is
                   VERB

_____ !
   ADJECTIVE

MAD LIBS® is fun to play with friends, but you can also play it by yourself! To begin with, DO NOT look at the story on the page below. Fill in the blanks on this page with the words called for. Then, using the words you have selected, fill in the blank spaces in the story.

Now you've created your own hilarious MAD LIBS® game!

YOU ARE
CORDIALLY INVITED

VERB ENDING IN "ING" _____

TYPE OF EVENT _____

NOUN _____

ADVERB _____

NUMBER _____

NOUN _____

A PLACE _____

ADJECTIVE _____

ARTICLE OF CLOTHING (PLURAL) _____

PLURAL NOUN _____

PLURAL NOUN _____

ANIMAL (PLURAL) _____

VERB _____

VERB (PAST TENSE) _____

OCCUPATION (PLURAL) _____

MAD LIBS®
YOU ARE
CORDIALLY INVITED

After _____ no clues in the Hall, you find an invitation
VERB ENDING IN "ING"

to Mr. Boddy's exclusive _____ on the floor. The invitation
TYPE OF EVENT

is printed on paper made from the finest _____ . You read
NOUN

the invitation, looking for clues . . .

Mr. Boddy _____ requests your attendance next Saturday
ADVERB

at _____ o'clock
NUMBER

for a private _____ party to be held in (the) _____ .
NOUN   _A PLACE_

Please come dressed in _____ attire:
ADJECTIVE

_____ with _____ are required
ARTICLE OF CLOTHING (PLURAL)   _PLURAL NOUN_

for all guests.

This occasion is for invited _____ only.
PLURAL NOUN

No _____ allowed.
ANIMAL (PLURAL)

Anyone who fails to _____ with these requirements
VERB

will be promptly _____ out by the household
VERB (PAST TENSE)

_____ .
OCCUPATION (PLURAL)

MAD LIBS® is fun to play with friends, but you can also play it by yourself! To begin with, DO NOT look at the story on the page below. Fill in the blanks on this page with the words called for. Then, using the words you have selected, fill in the blank spaces in the story.

Now you've created your own hilarious MAD LIBS® game!

MAPPING THE MANSION, PART 1

VERB (PAST TENSE) _____

NOUN _____

NOUN _____

PART OF THE BODY _____

VERB ENDING IN "ING" _____

ADJECTIVE _____

PLURAL NOUN _____

NOUN _____

NOUN _____

SOMETHING ALIVE (PLURAL) _____

ADJECTIVE _____

ADJECTIVE _____

A PLACE _____

TYPE OF BUILDING _____

PART OF THE BODY _____

OCCUPATION _____

CELEBRITY _____

MAD LIBS®
MAPPING THE MANSION, PART 1

Mr. Boddy was _____ in one of the many rooms of
  VERB (PAST TENSE)

Tudor Mansion . . . but which one? Get your magnifying _____
  NOUN

ready! It's time to investigate every nook and _____ :
  NOUN

- **The Hall:** This room is the _____ of the house and is
  PART OF THE BODY

  perfect for _____ . Take a moment to admire the
  VERB ENDING IN "ING"

  _____ _____ hanging from the ceiling before
  ADJECTIVE   _PLURAL NOUN_

  shaking hands with the suit of _____ near the door, which
  NOUN

  is made of solid _____ .
  NOUN

- **The Conservatory:** This room houses all kinds of exotic

  _____ (maybe even a few _____ ones!).
  SOMETHING ALIVE (PLURAL)   _ADJECTIVE_

- **The Ballroom:** This _____ room can make you feel like
  ADJECTIVE

  the princess of (the) _____ in her _____ .
  A PLACE   _TYPE OF BUILDING_

  There's even a/an _____ -painted mural of a Greek
  PART OF THE BODY

  _____ throwing a lightning bolt at _____ .
  OCCUPATION   _CELEBRITY_

MAD LIBS® is fun to play with friends, but you can also play it by yourself! To begin with, DO NOT look at the story on the page below. Fill in the blanks on this page with the words called for. Then, using the words you have selected, fill in the blank spaces in the story.

Now you've created your own hilarious MAD LIBS® game!

LOST IN THE DARK

ADJECTIVE _____

VERB _____

VERB ENDING IN "ING" _____

NOUN _____

PART OF THE BODY _____

ADJECTIVE _____

TYPE OF FOOD _____

VERB _____

PLURAL NOUN _____

PART OF THE BODY _____

VERB (PAST TENSE) _____

NOUN _____

VERB _____

ANIMAL _____

ADJECTIVE _____

NOUN _____

ADJECTIVE _____

MAD LIBS

LOST IN THE DARK

After finding no clues in the Conservatory, you hear a/an _____
                                                            ADJECTIVE

craaaaash and duck into a secret passageway to . . . the Lounge! You run

into the darkened room and click on your trusty _____-light,
                                                     VERB

revealing Mr. Green _____ the revolver! "What are
                    VERB ENDING IN "ING"

you doing with that loaded _____?" you demand. Mr. Green
                               NOUN

looks down at his _____ and drops the gun like it's a/an
                  PART OF THE BODY

_____ _____. "It's not what you _____,"
   ADJECTIVE   TYPE OF FOOD   VERB

he explains. "At the time of the murder, I was in the Lounge looking

for Mr. Boddy's collection of priceless _____. But it was so
                                        PLURAL NOUN

dark in here, I couldn't see my hand in front of my _____.
                                                    PART OF THE BODY

Then I got scared and accidentally _____ this display
                                   VERB (PAST TENSE)

case over. I was picking things up when you came in and shined that

flash-_____ in my eyes. You have to _____ me! I
         NOUN   VERB

may be a scaredy-_____, but I'm no _____-blooded
                    ANIMAL   ADJECTIVE

_____." You cross out Mr. Green's name in your detective's
   NOUN

notebook. He's got a/an _____ alibi.
                        ADJECTIVE

From CLUE MAD LIBS® • © 2020 Hasbro. Published by Mad Libs,
an imprint of Penguin Random House LLC.

MAD LIBS® is fun to play with friends, but you can also play it by yourself! To begin with, DO NOT look at the story on the page below. Fill in the blanks on this page with the words called for. Then, using the words you have selected, fill in the blank spaces in the story.

Now you've created your own hilarious MAD LIBS® game!

A SLIPPERY ALIBI

ADVERB _____

NOUN _____

PART OF THE BODY _____

ADJECTIVE _____

TYPE OF CONTAINER _____

TYPE OF LIQUID _____

NOUN _____

PART OF THE BODY _____

SILLY WORD _____

ADJECTIVE _____

VERB (PAST TENSE) _____

NOUN _____

ARTICLE OF CLOTHING _____

VERB ENDING IN "ING" _____

SAME TYPE OF LIQUID _____

NOUN _____

ADJECTIVE _____

ADJECTIVE _____

MAD LIBS®

A SLIPPERY ALIBI

You _____ watch Dr. Orchid, the brilliant _____
       ADVERB   NOUN

scientist, as she lingers in the Ballroom, holding a candlestick in her

_____ . "How _____ . . . and suspicious," you
PART OF THE BODY   ADJECTIVE

think to yourself. Then Dr. Orchid takes a small _____
                                             TYPE OF CONTAINER

out of her pocket and squeezes a few drops of _____ from
                                        TYPE OF LIQUID

the vial onto the _____ -stick. "Could it be poison?" you
                       NOUN

wonder. Suddenly, she turns her _____ and stares right at
                               PART OF THE BODY

you. "_____!" you scream, terrified. Dr. Orchid lets out
          SILLY WORD

a/an _____ laugh. "Surely you don't think I could have
     ADJECTIVE

_____ Mr. Boddy. I was here polishing this _____
VERB (PAST TENSE)   NOUN

with some olive oil when the murder occurred." Then Dr. Orchid

grabs the edge of her _____ and begins
                         ARTICLE OF CLOTHING

_____ the candlestick. "I always carry olive
VERB ENDING IN "ING"

_____ with me," she says. "It's a natural _____
SAME TYPE OF LIQUID   NOUN

polish. Aren't plants _____?!" You nod and quickly excuse
               ADJECTIVE

yourself. It looks like Dr. Orchid is _____ , too.
                             ADJECTIVE

MAD LIBS® is fun to play with friends, but you can also play it by yourself! To begin with, DO NOT look at the story on the page below. Fill in the blanks on this page with the words called for. Then, using the words you have selected, fill in the blank spaces in the story.

Now you've created your own hilarious MAD LIBS® game!

CLUEING IN ON THE CRIME

OCCUPATION (PLURAL) _____

PLURAL NOUN _____

LAST NAME _____

EXCLAMATION _____

VERB (PAST TENSE) _____

ANIMAL _____

OCCUPATION _____

NOUN _____

A PLACE _____

NOUN _____

COLOR _____

NOUN _____

SOMETHING ALIVE _____

NUMBER _____

PLURAL NOUN _____

OCCUPATION _____

VERB _____

MAD LIBS®

CLUEING IN ON THE CRIME

Okay, detective . . . you're halfway through the list of potential

_____ , deadly _____ , and rooms in
OCCUPATION (PLURAL)   PLURAL NOUN

_____ Mansion. _____! Let's review the clues
LAST NAME   EXCLAMATION

about the murder and suspects we've _____ so far.
                                                        VERB (PAST TENSE)

Mrs. _____ , Mr. Green, and Dr. Orchid, the _____ ,
         ANIMAL   OCCUPATION

all have plausible stories and have been eliminated. We know the

_____ did not occur in the Hall, the Lounge, the Conservatory,
NOUN

or (the) _____ . Mrs. Peacock had the _____ , Mr.
              A PLACE   NOUN

_____ found the revolver, and the _____ was with
COLOR   NOUN

Dr. _____ . None of those could be the murder weapon.
     SOMETHING ALIVE

That leaves you with _____ suspects, three weapons, and five
                               NUMBER

_____ still to investigate. One of them is most definitely
PLURAL NOUN

the _____ . Better get to it—this murder isn't going to
        OCCUPATION

_____ itself!
VERB

MAD LIBS® is fun to play with friends, but you can also play it by yourself! To begin with, DO NOT look at the story on the page below. Fill in the blanks on this page with the words called for. Then, using the words you have selected, fill in the blank spaces in the story.

Now you've created your own hilarious MAD LIBS® game!

MAPPING THE MANSION, PART 2

ADJECTIVE _____

VERB _____

A PLACE _____

ADJECTIVE _____

NOUN _____

PART OF THE BODY (PLURAL) _____

VERB _____

COLOR _____

TYPE OF FOOD _____

PART OF THE BODY _____

ADJECTIVE _____

VEHICLE _____

SILLY WORD _____

SAME SILLY WORD _____

VERB ENDING IN "ING" _____

ADJECTIVE _____

Here's some more _____ rooms in the mansion to explore, if
                   ADJECTIVE

you _____:
     VERB

- **The Lounge:** Located just across from (the) _____.
                                                 A PLACE

  This room looks like the perfect room to pour yourself a/an

  _____ drink, enjoy the _____, or kick your
        ADJECTIVE   NOUN

  _____ up and _____ a newspaper.
  PART OF THE BODY (PLURAL)   VERB

- **The Kitchen:** With its polished black-and-_____ tiled
                                                    COLOR

  floors, you're pretty sure no one orders takeout _____
                                                      TYPE OF FOOD

  when they have this gourmet galley. But did someone serve Mr.

  Boddy's _____ on a platter here?
          PART OF THE BODY

- **The Study:** It's so _____ in here, the cuckoo clock ticking
                            ADJECTIVE

  on the wall sounds as loud as a steam-powered _____!
                                                    VEHICLE

  But was the _____-_____ bird
               SILLY WORD   SAME SILLY WORD

  _____ when Mr. Boddy took his _____
  VERB ENDING IN "ING"   ADJECTIVE

  breath?

MAD LIBS® is fun to play with friends, but you can also play it by yourself! To begin with, DO NOT look at the story on the page below. Fill in the blanks on this page with the words called for. Then, using the words you have selected, fill in the blank spaces in the story.

Now you've created your own hilarious MAD LIBS® game!

BE A GOOD DETECTIVE

PLURAL NOUN _____

OCCUPATION _____

NOUN _____

VERB _____

NOUN _____

PLURAL NOUN _____

ADJECTIVE _____

VERB _____

ADJECTIVE _____

OCCUPATION (PLURAL) _____

NOUN _____

VERB _____

PART OF THE BODY (PLURAL) _____

VERB _____

ADVERB _____

PART OF THE BODY _____

ADJECTIVE _____

NOUN _____

MAD LIBS®

BE A GOOD DETECTIVE

A murder mystery has many twists and _____ . A good
                                    PLURAL NOUN

_____ has to memorize every detail of the gruesome
   OCCUPATION

_____ if they really want to _____ the crime! Keeping
   NOUN   VERB

notes in your spiral _____ about the colorful cast of
                          NOUN

_____ and their _____ weapons is essential.
   PLURAL NOUN   ADJECTIVE

_____ that list and check it twice! Never share any
        VERB

_____ information with other _____ , even if
 ADJECTIVE   OCCUPATION (PLURAL)

you think they're your best _____ . Remember, you can't
                                 NOUN

_____ anyone! Instead, keep all the suspects on their
        VERB

_____ by constantly trying to _____
 PART OF THE BODY (PLURAL)   VERB

information out of them. Listen _____ to everything they say,
                                   ADVERB

keep an open _____ , and remember that every detail is
               PART OF THE BODY

important, no matter how _____ it is. Eventually, one of
                             ADJECTIVE

the suspects will slip up and reveal a/an _____ that helps
                                              NOUN

solve the crime!

MAD LIBS® is fun to play with friends, but you can also play it by yourself! To begin with, DO NOT look at the story on the page below. Fill in the blanks on this page with the words called for. Then, using the words you have selected, fill in the blank spaces in the story.

Now you've created your own hilarious MAD LIBS® game!

ALL TIED UP

TYPE OF CONTAINER _____

PLURAL NOUN _____

NOUN _____

VERB ENDING IN "S" _____

SILLY WORD _____

ADJECTIVE _____

ADVERB _____

VERB ENDING IN "S" _____

PLURAL NOUN _____

EXCLAMATION _____

COLOR _____

PART OF THE BODY _____

OCCUPATION _____

A PLACE _____

NOUN _____

ANIMAL _____

VERB _____

NOUN _____

MAD LIBS

ALL TIED UP

While searching every _____ in the Kitchen looking for
_{TYPE OF CONTAINER}

clues (and finding nothing but stale _____), you discover
_{PLURAL NOUN}

a secret passageway hidden behind a large _____ . The
_{NOUN}

bookcase _____ open, making a/an " _____ "
_{VERB ENDING IN "S"}   _{SILLY WORD}

noise, and you sneak down the _____ tunnel until it leads you
_{ADJECTIVE}

to . . . the Study! Inside the _____ appointed room, you find
_{ADVERB}

Professor Plum holding a length of rope as he _____
_{VERB ENDING IN "S"}

near a table with a deck of _____ on it. " _____ !"
_{PLURAL NOUN}   _{EXCLAMATION}

you scream. "So you're the murderer, Professor Plum!" The professor

turns bright _____ and the hairs on the back of his
_{COLOR}

_____ stand up. "I'm no murderer. I'm a/an _____
_{PART OF THE BODY}   _{OCCUPATION}

at a university in (the) _____ . Besides, I was here when the
_{A PLACE}

murder occurred, using this _____ to tie back the curtain so I
_{NOUN}

could play a game of Go _____ in the moonlight." You have
_{ANIMAL}

no choice but to _____ the professor's story and move on with
_{VERB}

your _____ .
_{NOUN}

From CLUE MAD LIBS® • © 2020 Hasbro. Published by Mad Libs,
an imprint of Penguin Random House LLC.

MAD LIBS® is fun to play with friends, but you can also play it by yourself! To begin with, DO NOT look at the story on the page below. Fill in the blanks on this page with the words called for. Then, using the words you have selected, fill in the blank spaces in the story.

Now you've created your own hilarious MAD LIBS® game!

CHOOSE YOUR WEAPON

VERB _____

NOUN _____

ADJECTIVE _____

ADVERB _____

PLURAL NOUN _____

PART OF THE BODY (PLURAL) _____

ADJECTIVE _____

OCCUPATION (PLURAL) _____

PLURAL NOUN _____

NOUN _____

ADJECTIVE _____

NOUN _____

NUMBER _____

ADJECTIVE _____

OCCUPATION (PLURAL) _____

ANIMAL _____

MAD LIBS®

CHOOSE YOUR WEAPON

Which murder weapon would you _____, and what does

VERB

that say about you?

- **Lead** _____: Lead pipes are now banned because they

NOUN

cause _____ poisoning. You like to live _____.

ADJECTIVE .... ADVERB

- **Wrench:** Good for tightening _____ *and* loosening

PLURAL NOUN

people's _____. You're not afraid to get a bit

PART OF THE BODY (PLURAL)

_____.

ADJECTIVE

- **Revolver:** In the Wild West, _____ used these loud

OCCUPATION (PLURAL)

pistols. You like your _____ to go out with a/an

PLURAL NOUN

" _____."

NOUN

- **Rope:** Silent, but _____! You prefer having the element

ADJECTIVE

of _____.

NOUN

- **Candlestick:** Fancy *and* functional, candlesticks have been around

for _____ years. You're traditional and appreciate the

NUMBER

_____ things in life (and death).

ADJECTIVE

- **Knife:** The weapon of choice for stealthy _____

OCCUPATION (PLURAL)

everywhere. You're as sneaky as a/an _____.

ANIMAL

MAD LIBS® is fun to play with friends, but you can also play it by yourself! To begin with, DO NOT look at the story on the page below. Fill in the blanks on this page with the words called for. Then, using the words you have selected, fill in the blank spaces in the story.

Now you've created your own hilarious MAD LIBS® game!

SO MANY CLUES

NOUN _____

ADJECTIVE _____

LETTER OF THE ALPHABET _____

NOUN _____

VERB _____

ADJECTIVE _____

NOUN _____

LAST NAME _____

COUNTRY _____

COLOR _____

NOUN _____

OCCUPATION _____

NOUN _____

ADJECTIVE _____

NOUN _____

PLURAL NOUN _____

EXCLAMATION _____

MAD LIBS®

SO MANY CLUES

Cheerio, _____ solver! Did you know the original version of
                NOUN

Clue is from merry _____ England? The United Kingdom
                      ADJECTIVE

version (or U-_____ , for short) of this classic
                LETTER OF THE ALPHABET

_____ has the same rules as the US game we know and
    NOUN

_____ , but also has a few _____ differences.
    VERB   ADJECTIVE

For example, in the UK, the game is called "Cluedo" instead of

_____ . US editions of the game take place in _____
    NOUN   LAST NAME

Mansion, but in _____ , guests arrive at Tudor Hall. Some of
                   COUNTRY

the characters also have different names in the UK version. The British

victim is named Dr. _____ instead of Mr. _____ ,
                        COLOR   NOUN

and Mr. Green the _____ is called Reverend Green. British
                      OCCUPATION

Cluedo games also have different names for some of the weapons,

like "spanner" for _____ , and "lead piping" for the
                        NOUN

_____ _____ . But no matter what you call them,
  ADJECTIVE   NOUN

those _____ can kill! _____ !
        PLURAL NOUN   EXCLAMATION

MAD LIBS® is fun to play with friends, but you can also play it by yourself! To begin with, DO NOT look at the story on the page below. Fill in the blanks on this page with the words called for. Then, using the words you have selected, fill in the blank spaces in the story.

Now you've created your own hilarious MAD LIBS® game!

MAPPING THE MANSION, PART 3

PLURAL NOUN _____

ADJECTIVE _____

PLURAL NOUN _____

ADJECTIVE _____

NOUN _____

ADJECTIVE _____

NUMBER _____

NOUN _____

ARTICLE OF CLOTHING _____

CELEBRITY _____

VERB _____

VERB _____

PLURAL NOUN _____

VERB (PAST TENSE) _____

Time to investigate the last few _____ in this _____
                                    PLURAL NOUN   ADJECTIVE

mansion:

- **The Dining Room:** This room is adorned with sparkling
  _____ and _____ wallpaper. Too bad
        PLURAL NOUN   ADJECTIVE
  Mr. Boddy didn't get to enjoy his last _____ here.
                                               NOUN

- **The Library:** This is one of the most _____ rooms in the
                                               ADJECTIVE
  mansion. _____ dusty books line the shelves. There's
              NUMBER
  also a famous painting of a/an _____ in a yellow
                                          NOUN
  _____ that once belonged to _____ .
    ARTICLE OF CLOTHING   CELEBRITY
  Guess it's true what they say . . . you can't _____ it
                                                     VERB
  with you!

- **The Billiard Room:** There are so many games to _____
                                                          VERB
  in this room of the house. But just remember, it's all fun and
  _____ until someone gets _____ .
      PLURAL NOUN   VERB (PAST TENSE)

From CLUE MAD LIBS® • © 2020 Hasbro. Published by Mad Libs,
an imprint of Penguin Random House LLC.

MAD LIBS® is fun to play with friends, but you can also play it by yourself! To begin with, DO NOT look at the story on the page below. Fill in the blanks on this page with the words called for. Then, using the words you have selected, fill in the blank spaces in the story.

Now you've created your own hilarious MAD LIBS® game!

A WRENCH IN THE PLANS

VERB ENDING IN "ING" _____

VERB _____

TYPE OF FOOD _____

ADJECTIVE _____

VERB _____

TYPE OF LIQUID _____

ARTICLE OF CLOTHING _____

NOUN _____

ANIMAL _____

ADVERB _____

VERB ENDING IN "ING" _____

PART OF THE BODY _____

SILLY WORD _____

VERB _____

NOUN _____

VERB (PAST TENSE) _____

TYPE OF CONTAINER _____

VERB _____

MAD LIBS®

A WRENCH IN THE PLANS

You are _____ for fingerprints in the Library, but don't

VERB ENDING IN "ING"

find any. "Does anyone actually _____ these books?" you

VERB

think to yourself. Then, Colonel _____ runs through the

TYPE OF FOOD

room carrying a/an _____ wrench. You _____ him

ADJECTIVE / VERB

down the corridor, and he ducks into the Dining Room. His forehead

is dripping with _____, his _____ is

TYPE OF LIQUID / ARTICLE OF CLOTHING

untucked, and he looks like he's just been in a/an _____ with

NOUN

a mountain _____. With so few suspects left, you

ANIMAL

_____ decide to confront him about _____

ADVERB / VERB ENDING IN "ING"

Mr. Boddy. But the Colonel just laughs in your _____.

PART OF THE BODY

"Ha-ha- _____! I haven't killed anyone," he bellows. "I've

SILLY WORD

been too busy trying to _____ the leak!" The Colonel points

VERB

up to a spot where water is dripping from a long _____ in the

NOUN

ceiling. With another suspect _____ out, you decide

VERB (PAST TENSE)

to grab a/an _____ and help the Colonel _____

TYPE OF CONTAINER / VERB

that leak.

From CLUE MAD LIBS® • © 2020 Hasbro. Published by Mad Libs,
an imprint of Penguin Random House LLC.

MAD LIBS® is fun to play with friends, but you can also play it by yourself! To begin with, DO NOT look at the story on the page below. Fill in the blanks on this page with the words called for. Then, using the words you have selected, fill in the blank spaces in the story.

Now you've created your own hilarious MAD LIBS® game!

DON'T REVEAL YOUR SECRETS

ADJECTIVE _____

PLURAL NOUN _____

OCCUPATION _____

VERB _____

PLURAL NOUN _____

PART OF THE BODY (PLURAL) _____

VERB _____

NOUN _____

ADJECTIVE _____

PART OF THE BODY _____

PLURAL NOUN _____

VERB _____

ADJECTIVE _____

ADJECTIVE _____

MAD LIBS®
DON'T REVEAL
YOUR SECRETS

Want to be a/an _____ Clue champion? Follow these
                          ADJECTIVE

_____ to learn how to play like a/an _____ :
PLURAL NOUN   OCCUPATION

*   Never _____ your clues to anyone! A player's entire
              VERB

    strategy often hinges on the _____ in their hand. They
                                    PLURAL NOUN

    are meant for your _____ only!
                        PART OF THE BODY (PLURAL)

*   Learn to _____ a good poker face. When you uncover a
              VERB

    new piece of _____ , be sure to keep a/an _____
                  NOUN   ADJECTIVE

    expression on your _____ at all times.
                        PART OF THE BODY

*   Trust your _____ . Good detectives have strong
                PLURAL NOUN

    instincts that _____ them in the _____ direction.
                    VERB   ADJECTIVE

Deduction and reason are vital, but sometimes a/an _____
                                                    ADJECTIVE

hunch is just as good.

MAD LIBS® is fun to play with friends, but you can also play it by yourself! To begin with, DO NOT look at the story on the page below. Fill in the blanks on this page with the words called for. Then, using the words you have selected, fill in the blank spaces in the story.

Now you've created your own hilarious MAD LIBS® game!

CLUE BY THE NUMBERS

VERB _____

VERB (PAST TENSE) _____

NUMBER _____

ADJECTIVE _____

PERSON IN ROOM _____

COUNTRY _____

VERB (PAST TENSE) _____

NOUN _____

NOUN _____

ADJECTIVE _____

NUMBER _____

PLURAL NOUN _____

COLOR _____

ADJECTIVE _____

VERB (PAST TENSE) _____

NOUN _____

ADJECTIVE _____

MAD LIBS

CLUE BY THE NUMBERS

Clue lovers of the world, _____! The board game Clue has
                                VERB

been _____ by generations of players. It just celebrated
      VERB (PAST TENSE)

its _____-year anniversary! Here are some _____ facts
     NUMBER   ADJECTIVE

you might (or might not!) have already sleuthed out:

• The game was invented by _____ and Elva Pratt in
                            PERSON IN ROOM

  _____ and first sold in 1949. The Pratts originally
   COUNTRY

  _____ the game as a way to help pass the
   VERB (PAST TENSE)

  _____ during World _____ II. Despite the game's
   NOUN   NOUN

  _____ international success, the Pratts sold the rights in
   ADJECTIVE

  1953 for _____ British pounds.
            NUMBER

• The first version included additional _____, like a
                                         PLURAL NOUN

  bomb, an ax, and poison.

• Dr. Orchid replaced Mrs. _____ in 2016. She's the first
                            COLOR

  _____ character in sixty-seven years!
   ADJECTIVE

• In 2017, Clue was _____ into the National
                     VERB (PAST TENSE)

  Toy Hall of Fame. The board game has inspired a film, a/an

  _____ series, and many _____ books.
   NOUN   ADJECTIVE

From CLUE MAD LIBS® • © 2020 Hasbro. Published by Mad Libs,
an imprint of Penguin Random House LLC.

MAD LIBS® is fun to play with friends, but you can also play it by yourself! To begin with, DO NOT look at the story on the page below. Fill in the blanks on this page with the words called for. Then, using the words you have selected, fill in the blank spaces in the story.

Now you've created your own hilarious MAD LIBS® game!

TO THE CELLAR!

PART OF THE BODY _____

PLURAL NOUN _____

EXCLAMATION _____

NOUN _____

VERB (PAST TENSE) _____

NOUN _____

ADJECTIVE _____

VERB _____

VERB ENDING IN "S" _____

ANIMAL _____

LAST NAME _____

VERB ENDING IN "ING" _____

NOUN _____

PART OF THE BODY _____

ADJECTIVE _____

NOUN _____

VERB _____

NOUN _____

MAD LIBS

TO THE CELLAR!

With your list of clues in your _____ , you run to the
                                    PART OF THE BODY

Cellar. You push your way past a few spider-_____
                                              PLURAL NOUN

(_____ !) and shut the _____ so you can check
   EXCLAMATION   NOUN

your list without being _____ on by anyone. You realize
                        VERB (PAST TENSE)

there's only one suspect, one room, and one _____ left on
                                              NOUN

your list . . . Miss Scarlet in the Billiard Room with the _____
                                                            ADJECTIVE

pipe! You've used your skills of deduction to _____ the killer!
                                                VERB

Just then, Miss Scarlet _____ out of the shadows like
                        VERB ENDING IN "S"

a/an _____. "Okay, I admit it! I killed Mr. _____!
      ANIMAL   LAST NAME

He won when we were _____ a game of billiards,
                     VERB ENDING IN "ING"

and I got so mad that I pulled a lead _____ out from under
                                       NOUN

the bathroom sink and whacked him on the _____ with it.
                                          PART OF THE BODY

I guess I've always been kind of a/an _____ loser. Oh, and I
                                       ADJECTIVE

think that broken pipe might have caused a/an _____." It's
                                               NOUN

time to take Miss Scarlet to _____ herself in to the police.
                              VERB

_____ closed.
   NOUN

From CLUE MAD LIBS® • © 2020 Hasbro. Published by Mad Libs,
an imprint of Penguin Random House LLC.